Alessio Zanelli, Italian, has long ... age. His
work has appeared in over 180 ... His last
original full collection, titled *Th*... 2019 by
Greenwich Exchange Publishing ... Stanza
Representative for the Poetry Society of London.

ALSO BY ALESSIO ZANELLI

Loose Sheets
Small Press Verse & Poeticonjectures
33 Poesie / 33 Poems
Straight Astray
Over Misty Plains
The Secret Of Archery
Ghiaccielo / Skyce

Alessio Zanelli

AMALGAM

AMALGAM
Alessio Zanelli

www.alessiozanelli.it

Cyberwit
HIG 45, Kaushambi Kunj
Kalindipuram
Allahabad – 211011 (U.P.)
India

www.cyberwit.net
info@cyberwit.net

ISBN 978-93-90601-92-9

Cover image: *Golden Tears* (detail), 2020, acrylic and gold oxide pigments on canvas, 60 x 40 cm, by Andrea Schiavetta (courtesy of Leonardo Iacovino)

to anybody listening

Half of what I say is meaningless;
but I say it so that the other half may reach you.

KHALIL GIBRAN

ACKNOWLEDGMENTS

All the poems in this chapbook have first appeared or are forthcoming in the following magazines:

Artemis, California Quarterly, The Heartland Review, North Dakota Quarterly, Sanskrit, The Society of Classical Poets, Songs of Eretz, The Stray Branch and *Tipton Poetry Journal* in the USA;

A New Ulster, BFS Horizons, Focus, Here Comes Everyone and *The Journal* in the UK;

Quadrant in Australia;

The Nashwaak Review and *Nunum* in Canada;

Paris/Atlantic in France;

Contemporary Literary Review India, Phenomenal Literature, Taj Mahal Review and *Verbal Art* in India;

Italian Poetry Review in Italy;

New Contrast in South Africa;

Mediterranean Poetry in Sweden.

The author and the publisher are grateful to Italian artist Andrea Schiavetta for the free grant for the use of one of his paintings for the cover image.

CONTENTS

AMALGAM

KURAMATHI DAWN

The morning moves in shouting like a desert.

An ear to the ripples
washing by the lagoon ladder,
the other to the waves
lapping onto the golden sandspit.

The eyes adrift
across the creased turquoise.

A silent prayer
to the storm looming north.

The swooshing breeze
grows to howling gale
as a pallid rainbow
gently bends beyond the pier.

And sluggish time all of a sudden slips away.

EVERNAUTS

Sailing always west,
constantly a league
ahead of the terminator,
just makes sunrise eternal,
buys evernauts no time.
The sea looks boundless
simply as bent around a globe,
but some dry land at last arrives
to break the route to dream.
Even long before Pythagoras,
Jason knew that well,
his sunrise the golden fleece
while seemingly chasing it
he tried to escape instead,
for he also knew too well
all it would bring along
was the voyage's end.

SEACLOCK

Shimmer.

Over and over
on to just more shimmer.

Brackish spray on eyelashes,
heartbeat and breathing silenced,
frown on face and lump in throat
dying down to appeasement.

Staring at infinity
blinking back
at littleness.

Unceasing, assuaging, enslaving,
wombal gurgle, ancestral maker,
the sound of breakers is all that
confers overt existence on time.

On a strand
as anywhere else.

Ever.

SEAFARER
In The Wake Of Columbus

They have been teaching me all that it takes
to stand the ride, go far and make it worth
the strain and pain of often being alone
since when I was a toddling feeble child,
before I even learned to say my name.
No special skills but open-mindedness,
then wisdom, brawn and hunger most of all
I should have always brought along with me
wherever I would later find myself:
across dry land, at sea, above the clouds.
A boy adrift in tales of any kind,
I fell in love with depths of earth and space,
devouring books by London, Verne and Clarke,
afraid that water may have stayed a dream,
for early nightmares can be hardly killed.
Such fear turned out to be completely wrong
and soon I mastered tempests, whirls and streams,
as sure as I'd been taming peaks and stars,
aware of how real life can merge with dreams
until a day—a man—it all cleared up,
and I could easily tell the two apart:
undoubtful, reckless, restless, smart, secure.
Meanwhile I had embraced new ways to try
to conquer freedom looking for some place,
to understand the how and when and why,
by turning from the grandly vast or far
to what is hugely small and inly close.
My latest heroes Heisenberg and Bohr
had flung me through uncertainty and chance,
my novel trips had scattered me among
transparent leptons matching colored quarks,
elusive bosons, steadfast fermions, strings,
then deeper in and out till back to start:
Big Bang, inflation, cooling down, collapse?
Lemaître, Friedmann, Bondi, Penrose, Guth.
So long a journey just to go nowhere,

to come full circle time and time again,
as nothing is the way I thought it was!
I now realize that every quest is vain,
there's none to blindly trust or give in to,
but each and all to probe and sample from.
If born to voyage, what I'm left to choose
is only by which means, and never where,
for what, how long or in how many stops.
In all these years I've walked, I've run, I've climbed,
I've flown on airplanes, rockets, astral arks,
but first and foremost I have crossed the seas.
I've been commander, sailor, deck boy, slave,
from port to port around the globe and back,
then further off, on every kind of ship.
And since nobody can be really free,
for either dice or given laws do rule,
on top of foamy crests I want to be,
forever over such unboundedness:
unmarked and level, absolutely plain.
I've had enough of roads and charted routes,
of flying paths as well as mental ones,
of all that's certain, proven, set and safe.
I want to sail, reach out, explore, get lost,
my eyes already searching for beyond.
Just like Columbus did—no less, no more.

LAND AND SEA BREEZE

On the beach,
    the flight of the osprey
        in the eyes,
            portentous dream,
                I hope the wind won't fall,
    and the night
will come to meet me,
lost in the sand,
    to whisper the secret
        of infinite water.
           And if infinite,
                so is what springs
           from its depths,
        although it will end.
    Should the wind,
however weak,
    yet persistent,
        make it to the dawn,
            I'll have conquered life,
                and the chilly gaze
        of the osprey,
      still circling high
    in the amber sky.
And never a wave
    I could call the last
        will arrive,
           but the endless play
                of uprush and backwash.
           Me on the shoreline,
      just an image
coming and going,
land and sea breeze,
    to and fro
        like eternal thought,
           or fleeting wish
                on repeat through time.

APPARITIONS AT 5 PENNINE VIEW

Phantoms. Whether from the ceiling,
slanting, or from the floor, standing.
Greedy of heed, livid-faced, shades
neither light nor darkness will black
out. Me, spectator, expectant in awe,

not fear. Fear is of the dead. I am one
who can descry. On all fours, groping
in a corner, the eyes sealed, William,
after a vision, the missing one, fails
to recognize himself as it. Damned

like all accusers. Agape, the face
against a wall, unlike his mate the
eyes wide open, Edgar Allan shakes
with dubiety. The shadow or the soul,
the genius maybe, what he has always

obsess'd about. More and more unsure.
A widow's cap still on, afloat overhead
amid the room, not the Prince but the
crown Victoria's looking for. And her
cherished nickname, rather than the

Empire. Somber. A regular since he was
gone, I was but five, mad about his teeny
nephew, Uncle Lino pays a visit wherever
I am, provided there is a curtain through
which to peep. Static on the interior sill,

he watches over me, unseen. Happy.
Afraid of the others, perched on the
chandelier, skinny Alfredino grunts
he hopes some stronger hands will
pull him up, out of the well. Genuine.

None are funny, it's said. Untrue. Take
Neil, for one. He hovers higher than the
nanny, asking why on earth he has been
left alone to wander on the moon, where
his two comrades are. Disconcerted. And

there is Jon, who quit a few weeks before,
sitting on my bed, inquisitive-gazed, as if
wondering where the bloody keyboards
are, the Hammond above all, but never
speaks a word. Blue and angered. The

eighth and last of them, lying at my side,
silent all the time, really constitutes some
mystery. His quite old visage calls to mind
no name. I like to think that they can travel
either way, so that he could be simply me.

What they claim isn't clay, nor a passage
back, but something they were forced to
leave behind, or unfinished business of
some kind. Spooks seek no revenge or
redress, solely help and human touch.

AT THE END OF THE ROADWAY

Here, the end. No more lampposts
on the sides of the road, no
markings or signs. All strangely
exact and clean. No bushes
or trees in the abutting
fields, no overhead power
lines or poles of any kind.
All perfectly level and
smooth. After dusk it's next to
impossible to descry
the horizon, sky and earth
are one. A bit further on
from where I suddenly stopped
to think, as if I had lost
my bearings, another place
begins, where stopping doesn't
exist, there's nothing else than
perpetual motion, and
thinking makes no sense. I'm still
at a loss for a name for
such a place, but once I'm there
it won't matter anymore.

ABOUT COLORS

White is a byproduct of black.
Science says that.
It's simply evolution.
Lasting 8,000 years.
White can be good or bad.
Black can be good or bad.
Any color can be good or bad.
We all should come to terms with that.
Color ain't the issue.
Humanity is.
Acceptance of whatever color is.
Will you consent to that?
Either white or black?
Or any other color?
It all comes down to "will you be good or bad?"
Remember.
Lasting 8,000 years.
It's simply evolution.
Science says that.
White is a byproduct of black.

HATERS

They say I'm an insult to their unsullied world,
there's not the slightest reason for me to exist,
if I ever ceased to exist no one would notice.

They say my rights subtract from theirs,
my freedom of expression is a scandal,
I pose an intolerable threat to society.

They'd do a number on me,
they'd take me to the cleaners,
at last they'd kick me to the curb.

They say things inhumane, tirelessly,
although they don't hear what they say,
but at least they say what many just think.

KYOTO

The world's still turning. Faster. Upside down.
The Geishas keep on gaiting round Gion.
The headlines keep on blotting paper sheets.
The heat. Tornados. Landslides. Floodings. Droughts.
The timer's ticking. Treaties. Thunberg. Trump.

AUTUMN

Strata of flattened mist
begin to invade the soundless plain.

Long-emptied fields
and crops still waiting to be harvested
are slowly blurred away,
till dusk blots out them all.

The last migrating bird has gone,
perhaps the snow is not too far to come.

Assailed by gloom
and gripped by doubt
I check what's left
inside my crazy summer-end's
untidied secret drawer.

Cracked flakes of staling bran.
Dried drops of bottled brine.
Loose scraps of withered brain.

QUARANTINED

Headphones on, Sibelius's first
symphony playing, as I browse
through Tracy K. Smith's *Wade
in the Water*—being locked home
doesn't feel too bad. They all say
the air hasn't been so clean in fifty
years—what a joke that we must
remain indoors, like we've never
done before. Birds and beasties
can't believe their own senses. It's
taking quite some patience, but
it'll soon be over—they also say—
I prefer to imagine there's no hurry.
Everything will be back—social life,
trips, work, routine, pollution, din.
The same old frenzy. Do we really
think it's now we're going crazy?
Everybody can determine as they
see fit, I opt for my settee a little
longer—so reconciling and sweet,
no matter if indecorous or ironic—
placidly listening to *Karelia Suite*,
and waiting for my gin and tonic.
My way to wade the quarantine.

THE FLICKERING

The candle flame is not for always,
its flickering is.
A child, in our old, humble flat,
I got scared to death when it went pitch dark,
all of a sudden, because of a blackout.
Quite a usual occurrence in those days.
Therefore mom kept matches and a candle
in a specific place in every room,
although there was only one candlestick,
a cherished piece of patinated brass,
on a shelf by the kitchen window.
I miss that atmosphere,
that indefinitely lasting magic,
the quiet-voice chatting,
the Caravaggesque light
upon our faces around the table,
our gigantic shadows aquiver on the walls.
No house today holds candles,
kids don't know what blackouts are.
And yet the flickering goes on inside of me.

THE RAG

Keep me—*it seemed to say*—I'm not a cloth—when soiled or worn—to be dumped like this, without a thought. I'm not any rag—*it seemed to add*—one of those to be amassed in a closet corner, anytime ready to rub a floor tile or a tabletop, or else to be disposed of. Albeit cheap, my fiber is fine and tenacious at the same time, the fabric resulting from it is neat and uniform, perfectly smooth but—if the occasion arises—able to go deep, even to scrape. Yes, I'm an all-purpose rag, a universal cloth, such as you could never find again for all you strive to search for it. So, don't throw me away—*it seemed to reiterate*—only because you judge that I'm not doing anybody any good. I may really look like any piece of fabric, but I am not. Nothing easily discarded, lightly renounced, forever lost and thereafter unregretted. Think about it carefully—neither once nor twice but several times—then sleep it off and think again when reawaked. Above all remember—if ditched, there's no way to have me back, however desperate for me you may then realize you are.

RESURFACING

The blanket of years,
    dropped but unsettled.

Days to come along
    lying underneath.

About to resurface,
    layer after layer.

Tales to be rewritten
    if already written once.

All yet to be confronted,
    reviewed and rearranged.

Loose pages recollected
    and fitted into a finished book.

THE ARROW OF TIME

Her lineaments remind me of an angel,
although I've never seen one,
unless in some past life
I subconsciously remember.
I often find myself wondering about it.
Visions, déjà vu and premonitions,
do all such things make sense?
They say the arrow cannot be reversed,
that's an unquestionable law of physics,
a hard, undesirable rule of reality,
but it's only valid for matter and energy,
whereas remembrance is made of neither.
Maybe memories move through time,
I think they really do, both ways.
So, the angel I seem to recognize in her face
may be one I'll see in the future
or even in some other life to come,
whose recollection travels backwards in time.
That's how the arrow can be actually reversed.
That's how humangelical features hold me in doubt.

CALL UPON MYTHS

I'm lost.

Electra, Dionysus, Morpheus—
please help me
find where I come from
and go back there.

Only,
I mustn't
follow lights,
fall into ecstasy,
have dreams—
at night.

Just whisper in my ear,
make sure that I can hear,
deliver me from fear.

Do this and nothing else.

I'll do my duty
once you three do yours.

We'll all get our due or die.

THE LUMINARY

Prostrate, at the foot of the summit.
A crag over the valley on one side,
an outjutting rock face on the other.
Stuck on a ledge, at nightfall,
left with no option but to watch
the slow ascension of Venus
above the sharp horizon,
against orange and scarlet,
then crimson and purple,
up to full splendor over deep blue.
And to recollect the path traveled,
like that, as though in play,
until short of breath.
Knowing that, if destined for heights,
it would have been impossible
to climb beyond that observation point.
Alone.
The expanse, no longer regainable,
dark and silent below, on the clear side.
And the third brightest celestial body,
shining in comforting desperation,
to dispense one final glimpse
before the light goes out.
Infinity, reachless on high, on the blind side.

THE MIRROR

Tell me, man—
what is it you see in the mirror?
Is it the selves you've never been?
Both the one you wish you had
and the one you dread?
Or is it the one you're going to be,
whether you like it or not,
inexorably,
however hard you strive to run free?
No, it's none of those—
I think I know
what the mirror's sending back.
It's whom you're shedding behind,
piece after piece, day by day.
It's all you've been and done
and is forever gone;
all you've loved or hated,
fought for or been indifferent to.
It's your falls and rises,
crawls on the ground and soars in the sky;
your former neglect of the past,
contempt for the present,
defiance to the future.
It's the pristine effrontery of youth;
the mark you've made beginning to fade.
Yes, I know it all—
you linger there every chance you get,
reabsorbing as many flashbacks
as the glass allows you to.
And I just do because I'm you.

THE SWAN

Sometimes the swan believes it is a goose.
No harm done, it doesn't last long,
it almost always goes back to its old self
before taking flight.
It is when it convinces itself
it is a puissant raven—
while swimming in the pond,
afloat on such a queer assurance,
and a real raven whizzes in front of it
skimming the water—
that the problem arises.
Because then it wonders
why it cannot fly as nimbly and fast.
It often takes quite a few days
for it to repossess its identity,
but it can happen
that it never makes it again.
Eventually, evidence wipes out any doubt.
In fact, it stares at its own reflected image
ineluctably day after day
and every time it sees a swan
just below the surface
in turn looking it in the eyes
and wearing the typical fearful expression
of one that's met the ugly gaze of a raven.

SINKHOLE

●
just
to allow a
glimpse of how
the swallow works and
let the unnamed dread grow
too big to conquer a thread of bleak
light hard squeeze of night creeps through
cracks into the secret void where soul appendages
contort and struggle to plug its own bores from which fast
trickles keep on leaking out and falling to the bottom meanwhile
running dark to feed the obscurity creating an abyss so deep as to become
unclimbable by anything incapable of setting fire to itself or giving birth to a star

THE CLOCKMASTER

And so the Clockmaster
came to terms with it,
in the end at close quarters
with no one but himself,
to make the ultimate decision,
yet the very first at all.
He pondered what to do,
which one would be the final turn,
on which cog everything would stop.
Once again he beheld
all that was placed out there—
apparently still, mostly emptiness.
For one last time his eyes embraced
the whole of it, and every bit,
working out what his next move would be,
realizing how beautiful it was,
if quickly fading away the tick.
He thought, on and on, to the full,
then sighed and saw—the world,
and under its skin a skull.

THE TOLL

I've heard it thousands of times,
but I will miss the unmissable one.
That's why I stare into the night sky,
every time I hear it in the distance,
a cool warning, a dire housecall.

I'd like to bite the big one alone,
not be forced to vanish in droves.
And after attending some big show,
such as, say, Betelgeuse exploding,
a bit before Sgr A* swallows it all.

COSMIC NEMESIS

Somewhere amid the eons, a micro black hole
peeped at the edge of the solar system,
probably overlooked, certainly ignored.
The sun continued shining, unperturbed,
tirelessly fusing hydrogen into helium,
as it had been used to doing for billions of years.

The tiny visitor advanced,
slow but unswayed by any gravitational pull
along the plane of the ecliptic,
heading straight to the fulgent center,
invisibly majestic, totally undisturbed,
not the slightest wake behind it.

Without even realizing it,
from first to last
all the planets were swallowed,
just like every minor body,
silently, one by one,
as if with a snap of spacetime.

And not even when it came to be its turn
the sun, aglow from time immemorial,
worried about the minuscule orb,
reducing quickly, inexorably,
eventually disappearing
annihilated inside it.

One less point of light
now dots the stupendous galaxy,
its absence unnoticed,
as the sight-escaping devourer of worlds
proceeds on its endless path
to where it all began.